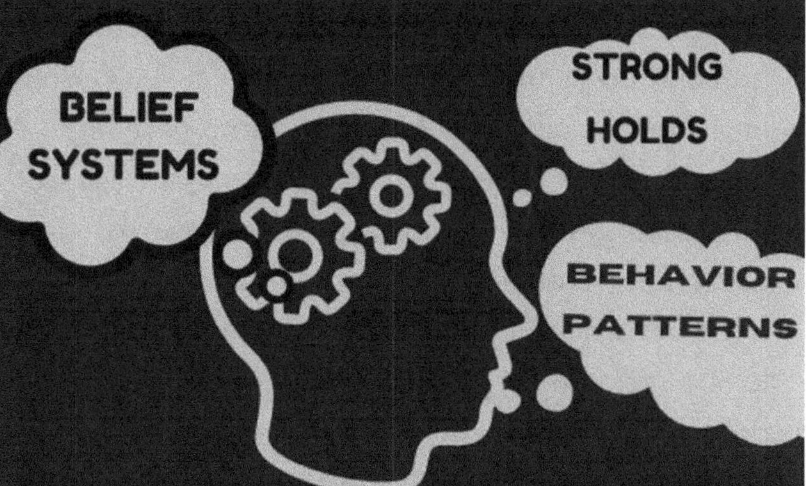

UNLOCKING MINDSET TRAPS

The Mindset to Handle Mental Warfare

DR. LAURETTA PICKETT

Edited by Anthony Ambrogio

Published by G Publishing LLC

ISBN: 979-888831906-2

Library of Congress Control Number: 2024912403

Published and Printed in the United States of America

DEDICATIONS

First, I dedicate this book to you, God, for giving me the wisdom to write and trusting me with Your word. Your Daughter Lauretta

TO MY SONS, I LOVE YOU ALWAYS

To my two sons, John and Norman. Thank you for your love, support, and also sacrifice during my teaching and travels. You both have so much wisdom and knowledge that the world need. I have traveled many miles where ever I am you both stay in my heart. My prayer is you both finish your God given purpose in life. These words will live a lifetime reminding you both there is no one on Earth I love more than you.   I Love You!!!

I thank my mother and father, for believing in me. I want to dedicate this book to my family, to my five grandchildren, and one great granddaughter, my brothers, my sister, and a host of nieces, nephews, cousins, and friends   **I LOVE YOU**

DEDICATIONS

PASTOR DEBRA BLACKSHEAR

Pastor Debra and I began as friends when we were kids. Our relationship grew from friends to sisters, then we had the blessing of pastoring God Is Real together. We overcame every problem with unity. Your love, support and leadership made this day possible. I will love you always!

PASTOR LORIE SMITH

Pastor Lorie, I've witnessed your journey from a teenager to a beautiful woman of God. It's truly a blessing to see your growth, teaching and training. We will be waiting for your books, you are an awesome teacher. Your mother would be so amazed to see the woman you have become. God has filled a void of wanting son's and daughters, by giving me many daughters like you, I love you.

GOD IS REAL INTERNATIONAL MINISTRIES

There is no one like you. Your diligence, perseverance, loyalty, and long-term commitment make you an unstoppable force. Every storm you have faced, you fought through like true warriors, yet with such compassion. I see each of you as part of a mighty Gideon army. Thank you for loving God and for believing in me. I love you all to life.

COVERINGS and MANTLES

APOSTLE R. D. HENTON: In 1982, after I accepted the call from God, I began soul winning and ministering. Apostle R. D. Henton counseled me and confirmed that I should obey God's call. He periodically called to encourage me as I traveled. I enjoyed visiting and hearing him preach. He would say, "I cannot hinder you by staying here." This was a man of God who encourage me to fulfill the call. He called me one day and said, "I told you I would not forget you." and began asking me to speak for Monument of Faith, where now his son, Apostle Mark Henton, is Senior Pastor.

APOSTLE C. TURNER: After years of being ordained and pastoring, I had the opportunity to work with Apostle C. Turner, who humorously provided me with a second set of credentials, saying, "I am going to cover you and broadcast on T.V that you're not alone." He ordained me on national television to give me endorsement. However, he immediately laughed, saying "I would love to let you work here, but I know you have to go." Apostle Turner frequently reached out to encourage our church and would call me to preach at Liberty Temple full Gospel Church.

PASTOR E. R. ALLEN: Pastor Allen was a mentor. I would watch her on tv and be so encouraged to see a woman doing what God was showing me. I had no living example of a female minister until I met her. I would study Katherine Kuhlman, but she was no longer with us. Then I met the beautiful woman who sings "JESUS—there is something about His name." She dressed beautifully and was so anointed. Pastor Allen's daughter, Dr. Lynda Allen

Washington, is now filming her mother's life story and asked me to play the role of Pastor E.R. Allen. What an honor! I remember Pastor Allen laying hands on me in the '80s, saying, "If you only knew how God will use you."

APOSTLE C. BUSH: Apostle Bush and his family have been a covering and a rock to me, my family, and church. He has been here through most of it all. He is not last because of what he means to me; it's just the order of leaders who I met first. I met Apostle Bush in the '90s, and even until now he is still the same. Day or night, he has wisdom. Apostle Bush has encouraged me to minister, to utilize the gifts in me. His counsel is sound. He asks, "Do you want the long or short version of your answer?" Sometimes I take the long version, because along the way you get such wisdom.

APOSTLE A. TETSOLA: Many years later I received mentorship from Apostle A. Tetsola. His ability to teach the word of God with revelation and to write books with his prophetic edge is outstanding. I received a second ordination to the office of Prophetess at his church in New York. Apostle Tetsola and his wife have done tremendous work all over the world. The revelation God has given him is supernatural.

APOSTLES AND PASTORS around the world: there are too many to name. Thank you for trusting me to bring God's word to your churches.

Words from the Author's Older Son, John:

I am the older son and have witnessed both sides of my mother's life—the struggles and journey from unsaved to saved. I am a living testament to where God has brought her from. She has dedicated her life to walking with God, loving her children, and helping others. The words of God and my mother are real. I was one of the first to read it, and not only was I proud of her, but I was amazed at how I could comprehend and apply her words, like using a dictionary. If you are striving to change your life for the better, read this book. The more you refer to it, the more it helps in life.

Words from the Author's Younger Son, Norman:

My mother is one of the most brilliant people you will ever meet. Her life experiences, along with her gift to retain knowledge, is truly a phenomenon. This book breaks down into the mentality needed to succeed and to navigate all aspects on the way. The balance of the mind, body and the goal of overcoming challenges are the foundation of this guide/book that will have an immediate impact on your life. I highly recommend this excellent read.

Table of Contents

INTRODUCTION

The world has experienced a pandemic, famine, and trouble of every kind. Many people suffered the deaths of family members and other hardships, and dealt with fears, which in turn caused trauma. Trauma has the potential to cause problems of physical, emotional and mental health—problems greater than we have ever seen. Trauma, coupled with wrong thinking, can create warfare in the mind. As a result of this warfare, fear, rejection, and paranoia can set in and control the way we think, building a mental fortress.

In the midst of the pandemic, I also saw something opposite happening: people began developing new businesses out of things they never thought of before. For example, instead of just wearing store-bought masks, many began making their own and then selling them, becoming very successful. Innovation in the world has rapidly grown.

Researchers have shown that there were more millionaires created in the shortest amount of time during the pandemic than at any other time in history. I saw God truly providing for us in the middle of trouble. There was a famine that some of us, while in the middle of the famine, never saw or experienced any hardship. God's glory was truly revealed.

I saw success and death operating at the same time; we experienced two opposites existing together. Satan has set up a strategy of deception for both sides, causing people to faint in their minds. The deception for the person who has experienced great trouble is, "You are a failure." The deception for the person who has been successful is, "You did this yourself." The purpose of this mental deception is to fog the mind not to trust God. Either you made it on your own, without God, or you failed because God was not with you. The mind, if not submitted to the word of God, will try and fight against the will of God and choose for itself. **Don't faint in your mind!**

Mental health is not limited to a diagnosis for psychiatric treatment, or a need for medication that serves to help many. Mental health is **SOUL CARE, caring for your soul**. The mind is part of your soul. A sound mind heals the soul. The many aspects of mental health provide what is needed to find peace of mind. This instructional book will mainly teach mental health from a biblical perspective.

1. WHAT IS A MINDSET?

"For as he thinks in his heart, so is he." What a statement from Solomon! Many times, I have heard people misquote this verse thus: For as he thinks, so is he." This reading is inaccurate. as it omits "in his heart." And, in this context, "heart" is more akin to "mind."

The word *heart* in Proverbs 23:7 is translated from a Hebrew word, *lev*. This word, *lev*, is often understood to refer to the innermost part of a person, encompassing their emotions, thoughts, and desires. In the Hebrew language, the mind is often associated with the heart, as the heart was considered the seat of emotions and thoughts. Proverbs 23:7 is therefore speaking of the mind. "For as he thinks in his *mind*, so is he." What you constantly think is who you will become.

Mindset is the eyes through which we view the world, shaping our thoughts, choices, and, ultimately, our destinies. Mindset is the master key that unlocks the door to personal development, your purpose, and fulfillment in life. The way we think today, whether our thoughts are right or wrong, our mind was set to maintain this way of thinking.

A mindset is the way our mind frames thoughts, and experiences. The thoughts and experiences we have govern the borders of our thinking. If those thoughts and experiences are locked (fixed), we will refuse to change the way we think. The locked position of our thinking will allow no thought changes; our mindset will monitor that thinking to maintain the flow of information and ensure that nothing enter and nothing exits.

According to Wikipedia, a mindset is a person's established set of attitudes toward someone or something. An attitude is a settled way of thinking or feeling, typically reflected in a person's behavior. This behavior can reveal, through a person's physical posture, what they think of a person or thing. The choice has been made, not according to the will of God, not what's right for us; the choice is made by how we are choosing to think.

We have to personally choose how to think, I remember, when I attended Englewood High School in Chicago, a police officer caught a group of us cutting class. He looked at me and stated, "You will never be nothing." In that moment, it felt as if my destiny had been sealed by the words of an authority figure, closing off the possibilities to fulfill my purpose. These words were familiar; as a child, I'd heard them, uttered by another authority figure. The words "You will never be nothing" rang in my ears, over and over again.

The words continued to silently ring as a small voice at every possible achievement. The words did not stop until I learned to cast those defeated thoughts down and replace them with God's words that changed my life: "Be you transformed by the renewing of your mind" (Romans 12:2). That's when I realized that God and I are in a partnership; there are things I cannot do that God can, and there are things God can do but, however, will not do, so I must. I have to cast down imaginations; I am responsible for interrupting negative thinking and exchanging it for the thoughts that will develop success in my life.

I had to give up defeatist words and negative self-images that some authority figure spoke to me. I had to listen and accept the words of a greater authority. This is why God said through Isaiah, "For my thoughts are not your thoughts; neither are your ways my ways, saith the Lord. For, as the heavens are higher than the Earth, so are my ways higher than your ways, and my thoughts than your thoughts" (Isaiah 55:8-9).

God's way of thinking is a higher standard of thinking. God does not lower His standard of thinking but encourages us to study His word to think like Him. We can intellectually think that our thoughts show how smart we are. But it does not matter who is impressed with our intelligence, If our thoughts do not serve the right purpose, we will be defeated by our own thoughts or by what someone else thinks of us.

Let's clarify a misconception: our mind is not our brain. The brain, while a crucial organ in our physical body, operates more like a watchtower. It monitors the body through our five senses (smell, taste, touch, hearing, and sight), but the mind encompasses much more than just the brain's physical and neurological functions. The mind includes our awareness, thoughts, imaginations, reasoning, consciousness, and subconscious. While the brain manages our physical body, the mind helps manage our soul, which consists of three main parts: the mind, the will, and the emotions.

Man is not just a physical being; he has three dimensions: he is a spirit, he has a soul, and he lives in a physical body. When we acknowledge only one of these dimensions, we limit the possibility of a full transformation.

For a full transformation, we must consider all parts of a person: spirit, soul, and body. Ignoring any part makes our understanding incomplete. A complete transformation of man, according to scripture, includes the transformation of the spirit, soul, and body.

- The Spirit of Man is transformed by becoming born again.

- The Soul of Man is transformed by the renewing of his mind.

- The Body of Man is submitted by discipline and humility.

Mindset vs Setting Your Mind

Mindset and Setting the Mind might seem just a reversal of words; however, there is a big difference between the two. A mindset can form purposefully through excepting or rejecting words, experiences, and emotions, we determine not acceptable. A mindset can also form passively living life, making no choices. It's a pattern of thinking that you never invited.

Setting the Mind functions in two main ways. One: we purposely accept truth and determine this is the way we will think. Two: we know what we should think, but our will is stubborn and we set our mind not to obey. Choosing not to retain truth in our thinking becomes sin in our soul. (Remember: the soul is the mind, will, and emotions.) If we continue choosing not to retain the knowledge of the truth, over time separates us from God, shown clearly in

Romans 1:28: "And, even as they did not like to retain God in their knowledge, God gave them over to a reprobate mind."

A mindset has set rules not to change unless something is determined important. If an intentional change is not made, the thoughts and mental pictures will stay the same. It is *we* who organize our set mind. Once we have determined right or wrong, that will be what we think.

I have heard many people say, "I have thought like this all my life, and I will die thinking the way I think." Such people are purposely forming the way they think, and it does not matter to them if they are right or wrong.

A mindset is formed in a combination of ways--mostly when our thoughts, experiences, and emotions repetitiously form to establish the way we think. When we look at the word *mindset*, it is our mind setting, to form the way we think.

When our mindset is established, we often switch to a default mode this mean we respond to situations automatically, relying on our deep-rooted patterns instead of taking the time to think things through consciously.

2. DEFAULT MODE BEHAVIOR

Default mode refers to the mental state or mode of mental processing that occurs when a person is not actively focused on a specific task or external issues. A default mode is often characterized by mind-wandering, daydreaming, excessive self-awareness, or spontaneous thoughts that arise when the mind is not engaged in a specific mental task. A default mode can also lead to creative thinking, problem-solving, and help with mental processing, that can help our thinking return to a productive place.

Example of productive Default Modes:

Amtrak Trains work on default modes; they can travel to many destinations that are determined by the tracks laid. Think of the train as the mind and the tracks as your thoughts. The train can only run where there are tracks. Thoughts, whether negative or positive, can only exist where mental space is given or taken. We grow or self-sabotage, based on thoughts we think. If we discipline our thoughts to think on what is good and productive for our lives, our mind will stay on the right track to success.

Examples of non-productive Default Modes:

1. Assuming the worst: automatically expecting negative outcomes because of past experiences.

2. Self-doubt: constantly questioning your abilities, worth, or decisions without giving yourself credit for your strengths and achievements.

3. Catastrophic thinking: jumping to the worst-case scenario in any given situation, leading to unnecessary stress and anxiety.

4. Focusing on past failures: hindered by past mistakes or failures without learning from them.

5. Comparing yourself to others: constantly measuring your own success, appearance, or achievements compared to others, leading to feelings of inadequacy and failure.

A Default Mode graduates from a habit to operating on mental autopilot, formed by repetition. This is the process: Habits are automatic behaviors that have been trained through repetition. This repetitious behavior forms a Default Mode which establishes A Mental Autopilot State, a state of functioning where we operate on a subconscious level. Our Default Mode, such as daydreaming, refers to the mind and brain's activity when they are not actively focused on external issues. Habit, Default Modes, and Autopilot are interconnected through repetitious behavior, which we will explore further.

I studied this area because I sought a personal transformation of my spirit, soul, and body. I wanted to understand how I could make my thoughts pleasing to God. I needed a transformation, and this can only come by renewing my mind through the words of God.

If you want to **stop the cycle of bad decisions**, we have to look at where they gain strength and how to stop them. My first suggestion to a person wanting to change is, **"Talk with God, (Prayer), get counsel**." My second suggestion is, "Let's begin with your thinking." Look in the Bible "for words of God to change the way you think. If I recognize that the person's problem is not a spiritual issue, I suggest they seek help from a doctor, in the proper field that can help them. Never be ashamed; get the help you need.

Unlocking Mindset Traps

3. OPERATING ON AUTOPILOT

A definition of Autopilot refers to a state of automatic behavior or decision-making in which individuals rely on routines, learned behaviors, or **subconscious** processes to guide their actions. When on autopilot, people perform tasks without **conscious** thought or effort. Habit and autopilot can be interconnected but are different. We can fully be aware of a habit, however autopilot is an unconscious state of behavior.

Autopilot can help with routine tasks but may lead to errors or oversights when tasks require greater attention. When I think of autopilot, I think of a type of sleep walking, moving without conscious awareness. Why is it important to understand autopilot? If we begin to intentionally allow God's word to program our daily test, we would develop an area in our lives that would create such success.

We dissect the terms; Habit, Repetition, Default Mode and Autopilot in order to study so we understand the process used to transform our thinking. This same process is used in scripture, "for the word of God is quick, and powerful, and sharper than any two edged sword, piercing even to the dividing asunder of soul and spirit, and the joints and marrow, and is a discerner of the thoughts and intents of the heart." Hebrews 4:12. Once are thoughts and behavior are on autopilot, its no longer a habit by repetitious behavior our thinking is now on autopilot.

Examples of Autopilot:

- A thermostat operates based upon an automatic return. If you set it to 70 degrees, no matter how the home temperature fluctuates—up or down—it will always return to where it was set; 70 degrees is the automatic return, the place programmed for the temperature to return. Our thoughts return to the place programmed unless we purposely change our mindset.

- When we drive, there are times we are not aware of turning right or left; we are driving on Autopilot. We even wake up at times and become fully conscious, aware we've been on autopilot.

The Subconscious Mind is on Autopilot

The subconscious mind is that portion of our mind that operates beneath our conscious awareness. The subconscious plays a significant role in shaping our thoughts, emotions, and experiences. It's a place where we secure longterm memories, experiences, values, and beliefs. The subconscious work continuously, day and night, to protect negative or positive thoughts and experiences that are not required by us to be removed.

Our subconscious mind operates on autopilot. It is responsible for automatic functions, such as our heartbeat, breathing, and digestive processes. Moreover, it's continuously absorbing and processing information, even when we are not aware of it. (Important to note: *even when we are not aware of it.*) The subconscious mind is a type of storehouse. Many of us go to our basement and find items we have totally forgotten about; however, they were stored in the basement, just waiting for us to return. In this same way the subconscious mind stores information with no change without your participation to reprogram it.

The subconscious is valuable to the person who wants transformation. The subconscious ability to operate on autopilot, gives us an advantage. I fervently believe the role of the subconscious has been neglected. When we are "born again," it signifies a profound spiritual transformation, the foundation for achieving true peace with God. In addition, God's desire for us is to be whole spirit, soul and body. The transformation does not stop with the born again spirit.

Many accept and nurture one part of themselves leaving a gap of emptiness, because the other parts are neglected. The areas of the mind being the conscious and subconscious are a neglected area that can bring transformation.

For us to witness a thorough transformation in our lives, a type of metamorphosis needs to occur on all three levels: spirit, soul, and body. This change can happen when our spirit is born again, our body is submitted and we are transformed by the renewing of our mind. One of the ways is to purposefully use our subconscious to operate on autopilot, but with information that transforms our lives not repetitiously cause defeat.

This transformation happens by Repeated actions, experiences, and thoughts "programmed" into our subconscious mind. Once there, they influence our behavior with our conscious knowledge. This influence can result in automatic responses and behaviors, much like how an autopilot can handle a plane's operations without the pilot's attention. The subconscious mind is one of the main areas we need to change in order to interrupt negative mental programming.

For example, you may drive to work and arrive without recalling each turn you made. This phenomenon occurs when driving becomes a subconscious activity that does not require your conscious thought. Consciously, you're thinking about your day, but, subconsciously, you're correctly navigating the drive to work.

The subconscious, or sub-basement, stores information from different sources for decades. I have remembered something I have not thought of in decades. An old song, a moment in time that I hadn't thought of in decades. Where did it come from? Those thoughts, old songs, and old memories are stored in the subconscious.

If the subconscious is filled with unwanted thoughts, moments of pain, and memories you no longer want to allow to control your future, *you* must remove them from your subconscious. Your memory will retain the information, but you will no longer operate based upon old information that does not serve your purpose and future. To remove negative information stored in our subconscious, we have to exchange the words planted in our mind. We can see this exchange spoken of by Paul, "Let this mind be in you which was also in Jesus" (Philippians 2:6).

Subconscious autopilot can be both helpful and harmful, depending on the behaviors or thoughts that have been programmed. We should not be afraid of the word programming, or the subconscious. Meditating on the God's Word day and night as stated in (Joshua 1:8), is programming our thoughts that we might develop what we meditate on. Repetition is one of the best forms of changing anything. Something done repetitively forms that behavior and becomes the way you behave and form a mindset.

4. REPETITION AND REPETITIOUS BEHAVIOR

Our mind is set by thoughts, experiences, and emotions. However, the process is formed by repetition. Repetition is one of the main ways to form a mindset. Repetition is repeating thoughts, experiences, emotions, and behavior over and over again until it forms automatic actions and responses.

Repetition is used to assist the memory to receive information and retain it. Repetition is used to form a mindset by constantly establishing the same information until you believe it, or simply accept it. This repetition can be positive or negative. Thoughts repeated over and over create repetitious behavior; we become what we consistently think in our heart.

Repetition and repetitious behavior can be great tools for memorizing, learning, and forming a good mindset that produces good behavior. Productive repetitious behavior can create great discipline, such as a daily prayer life, a weekly exercise regime, and any constant behavior that brings discipline and development to our lives.

Unproductive repetitious behavior creates problems. When we constantly repeat something that does not cause growth and development, we become stagnant and unproductive; we lose focus, and life becomes a cycle of the same failing events. Instead, we should use repetition to create a behavior that will help us fulfill our purpose in life.

Examples of Productive Repetition and Repetitious Behavior

1. A child learning to tie their shoe laces: repeatedly someone told them to make one loop, then another loop, wrap around the two loops, go in, and pull tight. This positive repetition can create development. Today, we don't need to repeat this process. We have learned, and have stored this information in our subconscious, and now it is on autopilot.

2. Studying for a test: you repeat repetitiously the answers to the test until they are sealed in your memory. It was not your memory that stored

the information on its own. The information was programmed there by repetition, and your memory held it, after hearing it over and over again.

It is crucial to have knowledge and understanding in order to expose and break free from mindset traps and avoid being constantly held back. In order to break free, we must stop engaging in negative repetitive cycles. One way to do this is by studying and understanding different repetitive behaviors.

Repetition can lead to the formation of both productive and unproductive behaviors. We have already discussed how mindset is shaped by repetition. When repetition is used constructively, it can establish discipline and help in our growth and development. However, when repetition is applied inappropriately, it can create cycles of wasted time.

Repetitive thinking or repetitively performing tasks, whether negative or positive, leads to the development of repetitive behavior. Different types of behaviors are formed through repetition. Let's consider some behaviors that are developed through repetition and assess whether we are actively shaping our lives or simply allowing each day to pass by under the influence of learned patterns of thought and behavior, whether productive or not.

Habitual Behavior

Habitual behavior is defined as habits that have become automatic and ingrained through repetition and practice. Habits can be both beneficial (such as exercise or healthy eating habits) or detrimental (such as nail-biting or an addiction). When we look closely at some behaviors, before we change them, we should determine whether they represent success or failure.

Habits are physical actions that are a response to an inward or outward programming. Habits are formed when we become familiar with certain behavior. Once familiar with a behavior through repetition, we form a habit. A habit will program us to continually do something, even when we don't want to.

Examples of productive habits:

1. Acknowledging God before making major decisions

2. Exercising thinking before speaking.

3. Eating a proper diet that ensures good health.

4. Looking for ways to change your life everyday.

Examples of non-productive habits:

1. Picking your phone up first thing in the morning, before taking time to pray or say good morning to your family. Scrolling through social media mindlessly, Spending excessive time on social media without a purpose, often resulting in wasted time and decreased productivity.

2. Procrastinating, (Putting off important tasks until the last minute, leading to shame, stress, slothfulness, and poverty.)

3. Overindulging in unhealthy foods. (Consistently choosing convenience or comfort foods over nutritious options can negatively affect your physical health over time.)

4. Oversleeping. (Consistently sleeping in late or not getting enough sleep can disrupt your daily routine and reduce productivity.)

5. Negative self-sabotaging talk, engaging in self-criticism or negative self-image

5. IMPULSIVE AND COMPULSIVE BEHAVIOR

The final behavior, that can involve repetition is impulsive and compulsive behavior. Impulsive and compulsive behavior operate by repetition. When there is any type of behavior pattern, there is a reason. Nonproductive behavior is created either by choice or by what many researchers define as impulsive and compulsive behavior.

Both impulsive and compulsive behaviors involve patterns of repetitive actions, but they stem from different underlying motivations. Impulsive behaviors are driven by the desire for immediate gratification or emotional relief, while compulsive behaviors are driven by the need to reduce anxiety or distress.

Impulsive behavior refers to actions that are performed spontaneously without careful thought or consideration of the consequences. Individuals who exhibit impulsive behavior may act on their immediate urges or desires without fully thinking through the potential outcomes.

Impulsive and compulsive behaviors are behaviors that can occur in all individuals, not just those who may require medication. We have to examine our receptive responses to non-productive behavior.

Examples of impulsive behavior:

(Remember there could be other reasons for these behaviors.)

- Making rash purchases—realizing later you cannot afford what you bought.

- Reacting impulsively in a fit of anger, without thinking of the consequences.

- Engaging in risky activities, such as reckless driving or substance abuse, without careful thought.

- Speaking without thinking, leading to saying hurtful or inappropriate things to others.

- Making impulsive decisions without gathering all necessary information or considering alternative options.

- Frequently changing your mind and plans you've made with others without clear reasoning, causing confusion and frustration for others involved.

Compulsive behavior, on the other hand, involves repetitive actions or thoughts that a person feels driven to perform, often in response to anxiety, stress, or a sense of incompleteness. Compulsions can create a sense of being trapped in a cycle of behavior that may be obsessive or interfere with daily functioning. Individuals with compulsive behavior may feel compelled to engage in certain behaviors to alleviate distress, reduce anxiety, or prevent perceived negative outcomes.

Examples of compulsive behavior:

- Repeated hand-washing or multiple-checking behaviors (repeatedly checking and rechecking locks, appliances, or other things to ensure they are turned off or closed).

- Seeking reassurance repeatedly from others about your decisions or actions, fearing negative outcomes if reassurance is not received.

- Engaging in repetitive body-focused behaviors, such as skin-picking or hair-pulling, to relieve anxiety or stress.

- Following strict routines or rituals that must be adhered to rigidly, even when they no longer serve a useful purpose.

- Engaging in repetitive mental rituals, such as counting or reciting phrases, to alleviate anxiety or intrusive thoughts.

Unless we have been diagnosed with a type of mental condition, when we unconsciously persist in behavior that is not productive, we are responsible for bringing change to our lives. We may need personal discipline, healing, and reprogramming of our thinking. Let us not forget we may also need deliverance.

I have seen many people cry out, "God, move this thing from me!" If this thing is in our control, *we* are responsible for changing it. Choose not to be alone in your development. If necessary, seek counsel to understand where you are and what blueprint you need to change your life. The cycle of non-productivity can be stopped.

6. THE STRONGHOLD

The dictionary definition of a stronghold is a well-fortified place that is designed to withstand attack and provide a secure place of defense or refuge. It is often a military term referring to a fortress, castle, or heavily guarded building. Figuratively, it can also mean a place or area where a particular belief, practice, or group is strongly defended or upheld. From my personal study in this area since 1982, I have found three main compartments of a mental stronghold are **Mindset, Belief Systems**, which create **Behavior Patterns,** linked by the umbilical cord of **Emotions.**

A stronghold is a mental fortress built around our thoughts, consciously or unconsciously. The thoughts can be negative and destroy our lives. Until we consciously make a decision to release them, nothing can move them. From my research of scripture, the main compartments of a stronghold are the following:

1.) **Mindset** as we have discussed, is a set of attitudes toward a person or thing—the mental position we think from. It's the mental framework that shapes how we interpret and respond to challenges, opportunities, and setbacks. We fortify the walls around the way we think in order to prevent change. Even if we are wrong, there will be no change because the mind is set.

You've probably heard the phrase "Talking to them is like talking to a brick wall." This saying illustrates how someone can build such a strong mental fortress around their beliefs. Some things will only change by prayer, fasting and releasing negative thoughts and confronting any external warfare, in order to change their thinking.

2.) **Belief Systems:** What we believe is the second part of a stronghold's strength. Our belief system forms the structured way we think; it's built from what we've heard, learned, experienced, or chosen to believe. Our beliefs act as a security blanket, grounding us and giving us a sense of security.

Our hopes, desires, and very sense of self are wrapped up in our beliefs. This is why, even if our beliefs are wrong, we often construct fortified walls around them. Maturity requires us to examine our thoughts, words, and beliefs. At some point, we have to take ownership of any misguided beliefs and commit to changing them.

Beliefs are an asset to everyone who use them properly; what we believe can literally save our lives.

Consider the story from the Bible of a father whose son couldn't speak and would throw himself into fire and water to harm himself. The father asked Jesus for compassion, and Jesus replied, "If you can believe, all things are possible to them that believe" (Mark 9:23). Jesus shifted the responsibility back to the father, emphasizing the power of belief.

A key point to remember is that you can change beliefs that hinder your success. What you believe about yourself—whether it instills passion to move forward or brings disappointment about your future—can ultimately change your life. You have the power to redefine what you think about yourself and, in turn, shape your destiny.

3.) **Behavior Patterns** Behavior patterns are the third component that gives strength to a stronghold. When our mind is set and we believe something to be true, this forms our behavior. Over time, the way we behave becomes a pattern. We can either be fully aware of these behaviors or, over time, come to accept wrong behavior as just who we are.

An example of behavior patterns can be seen in some children, in their behavior around certain children or adults. Their bad behavior is connected to a person or pattern of acting out. This behavior is influenced by a particular person or a certain environment: "Be not deceived: evil communication corrupts good manners"

(1 Corinthians 15:33).

The same child who is calm around you is now—totally out of character—jumping on your couch, screaming along with this other child. The behavior is different due to the influence of the environment or another person. (**Social facilitation,** according to Wikipedia, is the tendency for people to perform differently when in the presence of others than when alone.)

Behavior patterns are not limited to evil communication and social facilitation. Behavior patterns can form because of immaturity and demonic influence.

If we do not take the initiative in our life, we will be controlled by others around us and one day look up and realize, "I am not fulfilling my purpose; I just followed the crowd." We are responsible for our behavior and must acknowledge it if our behavior is not acceptable. We can surrender our body, our thoughts, emotions, and spirit to obey God at any time.

I know there are areas in our lives, we wake up one day, with more weight, or a thought, or behavior that make us wonder, "When did I allow this to happen?" This didn't occur suddenly; it accrued over time, day by day, while we repeated the same things, they were becoming **STRONGHOLDS.**

Types of Strongholds

Strongholds can be classified into a few different types, depending on the context—physical, mental, emotional, or spiritual.

1. Physical Strongholds:

Military Bases: Fortified structures designed for defense and strategic military operations. Historical castles, forts, and city walls built to protect against invasions.

2. Mental Strongholds:

Belief Systems: Deeply held beliefs shaped by our environment, culture, or just a stubborn way of thinking, knowing it's not correct.

Double Mindedness affects decision-making and critical thinking.

3. Emotional Strongholds:

Trauma Responses: Emotional defenses developed in response to past experiences.

Addictions: Behaviors or substances that a person feels compelled to depend on for emotional support. People with an emotional stronghold can allow their emotions to lead in every decision.

4. Spiritual Strongholds:

Demonic Influences: Demonic spiritual forces that control or oppress individuals, governments, and families for generations. A spiritual stronghold can dominate cities and nations; this influence can manifest itself in various forms, such as negative thought patterns, addictions, or destructive behaviors that hold people back from reaching their full purpose in life.

Sin Patterns: a spiritual stronghold can influence recurrent sinful actions or habits that hinder deliverance, personal development, and spiritual maturity. Every person is responsible for their actions. That said, sin patterns can be influenced by demonic forces controlling the minds of the people, through music, fear, false teachings, and many other tactics of Satan.

Paul identified Satan as the one **controlling the minds** of the people in his statement, "In whom the god of this world has blinded the minds of them which believe not, lest they would believe the glorious gospel" (2 Corinthians 4:4). We can look at certain areas in our cities and nations and wonder why certain crimes and bondage are more prevalent there than in other areas. In some situations, the reason can be a lack of resources, education, and training. In other situations, we clearly see a spiritual stronghold, influenced by demonic activity.

7. DISMANTLING THE STRONGHOLD

Dismantling in the context of strongholds involves breaking down fortified barriers, whether they are mental, emotional, or spiritual. The process requires a change in mindset, beliefs, and behavior patterns, all of which might have been deeply rooted over many years. The term "dismantle" generally means to take something apart, remove its components, or gradually eliminate it. We want every stronghold cast down; casting down is accomplished through the process of dismantling.

Dismantling a stronghold means taking apart and removing the negative foundations that support it, paving the way for positive transformation, and freedom. This process of dismantling involves perseverance, prayer, using scriptures to combat negative words, and, often, seeking and accepting help from sources that understand the battle. Such sources include spiritual counseling and any external sources that can help you navigate through the process. Dismantling and casting down thoughts and behavior require humility. Prayer with

Fasting work like twins, in unity, if submitted to will bring humility, this may take time

In Exodus 23:29, Moses wrote that God would not drive out Israel's enemies in a single year, lest the land become desolate and the wild beasts multiply against them. This same idea is presented in Matthew 13:30 in the parable of the sower, concerning the wheat and the tares. In that parable, it is said, "Let both grow together until the harvest; and, at the time of harvest, I will say to the reapers, 'First gather together the tares and bind them in bundles to burn them, but gather the wheat into my barn.'" The process of dismantling should not be seen as irresponsibly slowing down or complaining that we cannot achieve it. Instead, it is an honest acknowledgment of the process. It may take time.

Dismantle the stronghold with the same components that built it:

Mindset:

Change long-held, stubborn thought patterns or beliefs that may be self-sabotaging or harmful.

Adopt new ideas and ways of thinking that promote growth and the fulfillment of your purpose.

Beliefs:

Let go of false beliefs or misconceptions that you have accepted as truth and allowed shaped your identity and actions. Accept God's thoughts of you, and those who genuinely love you, but most of all discover your uniqueness and learn to love yourself, despite all your failures.

Behavior Patterns:

Break free from habitual actions or routines that reinforce the stronghold and may contribute to ongoing struggles. Develop new, disciplined behaviors and habits that align with your vision and purpose for life.

Examples of Behavior Patterns

Growing up in Chicago, we lived in a large building called "the Project," one quickly realizes that, while it was a blessing for families seeking a better life, because of the low income. I remember being excited we girls got our own room. Many of the residence used this time to get educated and moved on successfully, however, for many, it became a form of confinement. Whatever the project's initial intent, for our families were, many of the people did not become productive. for different reasons from hardship, gangs, lack of finances, and many homes lacked male role models. For some the mindset didn't shift accordingly, and their behavior patterns remained stagnant. For instance…

Many residence screen doors were missing. But, instead of repairing them or removing the entire screen door as many residence did, some simply stepped over the frames of the doors, laughing, taking the path of least resistance, while you would see others fixing the screens themselves. Seeking a better existence requires us to resist old, unproductive patterns of thinking, and behavior.

The familiar paths of lack, sickness, and failure are comfortable, but staying bound means accepting mediocrity. True change require transformation, and, for many, that begins with renewing our minds as stated in Romans 12:2: "Do not be conformed to this world, but be transformed by the renewing of your mind."

Our spirits may be reborn, enabling us to aspire to heavenly goals, in addition, living a transformed life here on Earth gives us a radical change in how we think, believe, and behave. Even when presented with clear evidence from the Word of God that their actions or thoughts are off the mark, people often hold on to their old ways, arguing for their familiarity and for remaining in their comfort zones.

Just because we've practiced something for a long time doesn't guarantee it is correct. Negative thoughts, limiting beliefs, and past failures ingrained in us require conscious effort to overcome. To truly change our lives, we must unlearn what we've adapted to and embrace the renewal of our minds and, by doing so, transform our reality.

Examples of Dismantling a Stronghold

2 Corinthians 10:3-6 offers insight into strongholds and how to dismantle them. Dismantling a

stronghold, while it may be influenced by external sources, is an internal battle. This scripture provides key principles for dismantling the power of a stronghold.

"For though we walk in the flesh, **we do not war after the flesh**. For the **weapons** of our warfare are not carnal but mighty through God to the pulling down of strongholds; Casting down **imaginations**, and every **high thing** that **exalteth itself** against the **knowledge of God**, and bringing into **captivity every thought** to the **obedience of Christ.** And having in **readiness to revenge all disobedience**, when your **obedience is fulfilled**." 2 Corinthians 10:3-6

1.) The first strategy to dismantle a stronghold is to remember that, while we live in the flesh, this warfare is not of the flesh. This battle is not physical; it is mental, spiritual, and emotional. Every battle we face should be approached with the name of Jesus, fully accepting what His blood has accomplished in our lives. We cannot rely on our five senses—hearing, smelling, tasting, touching, or seeing—to fight this battle. Regardless of external interferences, the victory is won internally.

2.) The next strategy to dismantle a stronghold is to recognize the stronghold: Identify the false beliefs, habits, or thought patterns that are contrary to the knowledge of God. This could be anything that holds a negative influence over one's mindset, belief, or behavior.

3.) The next strategy is to recognize the type of weapons needed. The weapons needed are spiritual weapons—not items like guns or knives, which are physical weapons. Unlike physical weapons, spiritual weapons include scripture, study, faith, and prayer. Prayer allows you to communicate with God and access His power of the Holy Spirit.

In Ephesians 6, the Apostle Paul describes the "armor of God," which consists of several spiritual weapons. Here are some of the weapons listed in Ephesians 6:14-17:

- **Belt of Truth**: This symbolizes honesty and integrity.

- **Breastplate of Righteousness**: represents living a life of moral integrity and right standing with God, based on the truth of His word. It is important not to fall into the trap of false doctrines about righteousness or to become burdened by human-made religious guidelines. Legalism—a strict adherence to religious rules and traditions without true spiritual connection—can become a stronghold that manipulates authentic faith and a genuine relationship with God. Instead, righteousness should be rooted in a sincere commitment to God's teachings and a daily relationship with Him.

- **Having your feet ready and prepared to share the Gospel of Peace**: This signifies being prepared to spread the message of peace with God and mankind: unity and love.

- **The Shield of Faith**: This represents faith in God, which can extinguish all the flaming arrows of the evil one. Faith is a protection, a shield to cover our hearts when doubt, fear and unbelief would try and dominate.

- **The Helmet of Salvation**: This symbolizes the assurance of salvation and protection for the mind. Salvation, healing, and deliverance give protection for the mind; however, they don't make us exempt from being responsible in our thinking.

- **The Sword of the Spirit**: This is the word of God, the Bible, used to counter attack lies and deception. Seducing spirits and doctrines of devils are prevalent in the world, and the only thing that can expose them is the truth of the word of God.

Additionally, Paul emphasizes the importance of prayer as a crucial part of the armor: Prayer, Intercession, and Spiritual Warfare: This involves intense, prayer and spiritual warfare, for oneself and others in the faith. The effectual fervent prayer of a righteous man avails much.

These spiritual weapons are designed to protect believers and help them stand firm against spiritual challenges. Ask for strength, wisdom, and the ability to see and confront the strongholds in your life. These have divine power to dismantle and destroy strongholds.

4.) The next strategy to dismantle a stronghold is to recognize, this is not only an outside enemy but the "inner me." Our inner thoughts, imaginations, and past hurts and disappointments can construct a fortified wall that reinforces familiar patterns and behaviors. Addressing an external enemy is different from confronting the inner self.

This requires facing the truth, not merely being hearers of the Word, but also doers of the same Word.

5.) The next strategy to dismantle a stronghold is casting down imaginations. To cast down imaginations is to remove negative and demonic images and thoughts from your thinking. This involves exchanging harmful thoughts and images for biblical positive ones. If unchecked, these negative thoughts and images can play repetitiously in your mind, much like a movie.

Imaginations not controlled can create fear and anxiety: Constant worry and fear can create a stronghold that prevents individuals from stepping out in faith and fulfilling their purpose. Fear can of course be a mental limitation. Fear can be a spirit; 2 Timothy 1:7: "For God has not given us the spirit of fear but of power, and of love, and of a sound mind." Imaginations can create a fear like an umbilical cord that binds the freedom and creativity of your thought life.

6.) The next strategy to dismantling a stronghold is casting down every high thing that exalts itself against the knowledge of God. This involves engaging in a mental battle with knowledge, words, and thoughts. In 2 Corinthians 10:5, the term "high thing" refers to any belief, attitude, argument, or ideology that opposes or exalts itself against the knowledge of God.

This includes anything that sets itself up against the truth of God and His teachings. Such high things can be our own ego, pride, or external influences that lead us away from God's truth. Taking these "high things" captive involves identifying them, rejecting their falsehood, and aligning our thoughts and actions with the obedience of Christ.

7.) The next strategy to dismantling a stronghold is to bring every thought into captivity to the obedience of Christ. This is form of mental and spiritual warfare, requiring us to engage deeply with our own internal thought patterns. Left unchecked, thoughts can evolve into imaginations and high things that stand against the knowledge of God.

To gain control over our thought life, it is crucial to identify, capture, and realign these thoughts with the obedience of Christ, rejecting any falsehoods that may try and gain dominance. Overcoming spiritual strongholds requires personal growth and maturity. It's important to recognize and address these spiritual strongholds in order to experience greater freedom, peace, and spiritual growth.

8.) The final strategy to dismantle a stronghold is "having in readiness to revenge all disobedience when your obedience is fulfilled" (2 Corinthians 10:6). Once we have fully committed ourselves to obeying Christ and aligning our thoughts and actions with His teachings, we'll be prepared and equipped to address and correct any disobedience or wrongful behaviors, both in ourselves and in others.

The readiness to "revenge" disobedience suggests taking decisive and corrective action against anything that stands contrary to Godly principles, to insure our own obedience is in complete alignment with God's words. Revenge requires us to resist, internally and externally. Overcoming temptation requires us to resist our thoughts internally and resist the devil externally, and he will flee. Binding and Loosing are external weapons, when Satan comes to temp us he cannot find anything in us to temp, this is why we must resist him, and his temptation, then he will flee.

8. PERSONAL DEVELOPMENT AND SPIRITUAL MATURITY

Changing the way we think requires personal development and spiritual maturity. While they can work together, they are different concepts. Personal development can be seen operating by the skills and talents we choose to refine, regardless of changes in our thinking or attitude. We can even study to develop our mind as famous scientists, creating breakthrough inventions, which is needed, however, this does not mean we are spiritually mature.

For example, someone with a God-given gift for singing or preaching can utilize these abilities without changing their integrity or inner character. The gifts and callings of God are without repentance—meaning, when God gives us a gift, He does not change His mind, even if we do.

Spiritual maturity, while it has a measure of personal development, it requires much more. Spiritual maturity involves more than just skill development. It requires a deeper transformation of the human spirit, lead by personal relationship with God, marked by integrity and the development of the fruit of the Holy Spirit. For those seeking to transform their lives, spiritual maturity demands growth in areas highlighted in Galatians 5:22-23, such as love, joy, peace, patience, kindness, goodness, faithfulness, gentleness, and self-control.

The gifts and fruit of the Holy Spirit are different. The gifts of the Holy Spirit are given to us not by our choice, by God's choice. The fruit of the Holy Spirit are developed through relationship with God and relationship building, we can choose to cultivate the fruit. They both are awesome, but have different roles in our lives. The gifts assist us to minister to others, while the fruit changes us by way of our character building integrity and respect.

Take some time to reflect on where you stand in both personal development and spiritual maturity. Assess areas where growth is needed, and be intentional about nurturing these aspects in your life.

9. FOR AS HE THINKETH IN HIS HEART, SO IS HE

As mentioned earlier, I've often heard people say, "As a man thinketh, so is he," but that's not quite accurate. The correct scripture is " For as he thinketh **in his HEART,** so is he" (Proverbs 23:7). We think many thoughts that never change how we think; thoughts alone do not change who we are. Some experts say we think on average **48.6 thoughts a minute**, which would average to about **70,000 thoughts in a day**. We don't become every thought we think.

There have been extensive studies by scientists, doctors, and even television programs that aim to understand the way we person thinks. These researchers examine thought and behavior patterns to predict future actions, though they can never get it 100% right. This is because no one can fully know the mind of a person except for God and that individual. There are even moments when we don't fully understand our own minds; only God, who created us, can truly comprehend them. Someone might ask the question why should I ask God about my mind and my thoughts? The answer is He gave us our minds and thoughts, He understands them completely.

The Different Types of Mindsets

The Bible provides insights into different mindsets and thinking patterns that can determine the outcomes of our behaviors. Introducing the various types of minds as described in the Bible can help highlight how different mindsets influence our behaviors and outcomes.

This may sound funny, but every mind belongs to someone, and directions come from how that mind thinks. When different patterns of thinking compete for control in a space that can accommodate only one clear line of thought, it leads to confusion and a lack of focus, causing mental conflict. Here is a list of different mindsets and ways of thinking mentioned in the Bible, beginning with a Double-mind.

The Double Mind

The term *Double Minded* comes from the Greek word *Dipsuchos*, meaning "a person with two souls" or doubled souled. The translation does not only suggest two thoughts; it states two *souled*.

The soul of man has three main parts: the mind, the will and the emotions. This would mean one person with two opposite mindsets, two opposite wills, and two opposite sets of emotions would have a hard time trying to go in one direction. A double-minded person has two different ways of thinking that are fighting for space where only one should live.

People with a double mind are not just indecisive; they are battling with two opposite thought patterns. Every one of us makes decisions, and sometimes we have multiple choices, but choices are different for a double mind. A double mind does not have multiple choices; it has two different processes of thinking that cannot co-exist and remain mentally stable. An example of this conflict of processes would be trying to turn a car left and right at the same time. James says "a double-minded man is unstable in all of his ways" (James 1:8).

A double mind is considered a double mindset. Remember: a mindset is the position from which you make decisions. When the Bible speaks of a double-minded person, it implies that the individual harbors two conflicting sets of beliefs, values, or attitudes, leading to inconsistency and instability. This dual way of thinking can manifest in various aspects of this person's life, causing inner conflict and unusual behaviors.

For instance, a double-minded person may waver between faith and doubt, or between spiritual truth and worldly desires. This kind of mindset prevents the person from fully committing to a single path or making firm decisions, resulting in a lack of clarity and direction.

A double mind creates a conflict between your spirit, soul, and body. This conflict is fought within the mind, creating a mental storm of worry, fear, doubt, and unbelief. A double mind is unhealthy; it results in mental confusion, leading to an unstable life. For stability, everything in our lives requires us to be sound-minded. A sound mind requires removal of all fear. Internal and External fears.

Consider Lot's wife in Genesis 19. She was clearly told not to look back at her old life in Sodom and Gomorrah but instead to walk forward to a new future. Her desire not to leave the familiar captured her thoughts, halting her future. In her mind, the past life, despite its sin and destruction, felt so familiar that she couldn't resist the temptation to look back and desire it.

She looked back and lost the promise of a better life. She was clearly double-minded, trying to walk forward while looking back at the same time. Make up your mind today to focus on the will of God for your life and don't look back. As my brother Larry once taught, use the rearview mirror only as a guideline. If you turn all the way around to see what's behind you, you cannot see what's coming. To walk into something new you have to leave the past. You cannot enter a new season without leaving the last season behind.

Being double-minded is the inner struggle within your mind, will, and emotions, torn in opposite directions. For instance, a double mind can form when you're in the midst of temptation, as you desire to live for God but also long for what tempts you. Recognizing this internal conflict is crucial, and, when faced with double-mindedness, it's important to pause and determine the right path to take. The next section will show some of the ways a double-mind is formed.

How a Double Mindset Is Formed

Unlocking mindset traps requires an understanding of the different mindsets mentioned in the Bible. A double mind can form in various ways. A double-minded person is someone who is indecisive, hesitant, or conflicted in their thoughts and actions. This state of mind can form for a variety of reasons, mainly due to internal conflicts, uncertainties, or competing desires.

Some factors that may contribute to the formation of a double mind include the following:

1. Conflicting desires or beliefs: When people hold conflicting desires or beliefs, they may struggle to make decisions or take actions that align with what should be their priorities. Take some time to really understand what you believe and why, what your desires are, and whether those desires will fulfill your purpose in life.

2. Fear of making the wrong choice: A double mind can develop when someone is afraid of making a mistake or facing negative consequences, leading to hesitation and internal conflict. A double mind can be formed by temptation. When we allow temptation to cause us to waver back and forth in our choices, a double mind can be formed.

3. Unclear purpose: Without a clear sense of purpose or understanding of one's priorities, goals, and vision, a person may find it challenging to make consistent decisions. Understanding your purpose can give you clarity of direction when making decisions.

4. External influences: Pressure from others, what's socially accepted, or conflicting opinions can contribute to a double mind, causing doubt and uncertainty. You can quiet external influences by prayer and also by consecrating some time away to get clear about what voices you are listening to.

5. Emotional instability: Strong emotions such as anxiety, stress, or fear can cloud judgment and lead to contradictory thoughts and behaviors. Defining your emotions can give great insight to where you are mentally.

6. Double-minded by doubt: A double mind can be formed by doubt. Doubt causes you to question yourself. When you question yourself, you become unstable in your thinking; there is no clear focus on what's real or not real. When you doubt, there is **no commitment** to a decision.

7.) Double-minded by Fear: A double mind can be formed by Fear. Fear has torment. Fear creates imaginations that give an illusion of something that's not there or that what's there has the power to hinder or completely destroy you. Fear causes us to have an inner conflict, not having the confidence to focus in one direction.

8.) Unforgiveness: A double mind can form by unforgiveness when you struggle between forgiving or holding onto the hurt, pain, and anger of what was said or done to you. This struggle to forgive will force you to have a double mind between right and wrong.

9.) Carnality: Carnality refers to the quality or state of being purely physical or worldly, particularly in relation to sexual appetites or desires. It is often used to describe actions, thoughts, or behaviors that are driven by physical or sensual desires rather than spiritual or intellectual ones. Carnality can create a double mind because of the battle between being spiritually minded and carnally minded. The carnal mind will always think contrary to the spiritual mind, creating two opposite thoughts.

The person with a double mind is in a place of mental compromise and temptation between good and evil, right and wrong, or simply two different choices, knowing clearly both cannot be the will of God.

Double-Minded Behavior

A double mind develops problematic attitudes, such as **double-gated**, **doubled-tongued**, and **two-faced**, which leads to problematic behavior.

- **<u>Double-gated</u>.** A gate is a place of entry and exit. A double mind has two different routes in and out of your thinking, creating not one route to your mind but two. This activity can develop many different behaviors based on what thought is being processed at the time.

- **<u>Doubled-tongued:</u>** A person with a double mind may express different thoughts without committing to either. Their words form from the many thoughts that fill their mind. Out of the abundance of the heart, the mouth speaks. If not controlled, the tongue can say hurtful things. On the other hand, when filled with gratitude, the heart can lead the mouth to speak words of thankfulness.

- **<u>Double-faced or Two-faced:</u>** A double-minded person often leads two separate lives, with their actions fluctuating based on their current thought process. The face they show to the world can change depending on which inner thought is more dominant at any given moment. This can result in behavior that appears inconsistent or lacking in integrity.

I want to make sure we remember a person working through double-mindedness could be a person really desiring to operate in integrity. This person may need our compassion to support them.

Overcoming a double mind begins with submitting our will to God's plan and gaining clarity on His vision and purpose for our life. Seeking wise counsel and considering spiritual deliverance. Fasting under medical supervision, can be very helpful. Spiritually, fasting does not necessarily move God; it helps us humble ourselves, putting us in a better mental position to make choices.

Establishing confidence and finding inner peace through prayer and the word of God has helped me resolve internal conflicts, leading to a more decisive mindset. In today's world, there is a growing awareness of mental health. Don't hesitate to seek support if you need it.

10. THE SPIRITUAL MINDED PERSON

A spiritually-minded person is one who continually aligns their thoughts with God's way of thinking. God's ways and thoughts differ from ours. Being spiritually minded is necessary for walking with God. We connect with God through our born-again spirit; however, our minds need to be renewed by the word of God because our minds are not naturally reborn.

A spiritually-minded person leads a different life-style, viewing and interpreting things through the lens of God's word. "For to be carnally minded is death, but to be spiritually minded is life and peace" (Romans 8:6).

When we experience transformation through the renewal of our mind, we gain the ability to think like Christ. This is what it means to be spiritually minded. It involves the union of a born-again human spirit and a renewed mind. This transformation through the renewal of our minds enables us to think like Christ. Being spiritually-minded requires this very transformation: a perfect combination of a reborn spirit and a renewed mind. The reborn spirit is mandatory for a spiritual mind.

What is the reborn spirit or human spirit, and how does it function?

So, How Does the Human Spirit Function?

The human spirit is how we worship and connect to God. Our spirit is the candlestick of the Lord, meaning it is the place that, by prayer, has light so we can find Him. "God is a spirit, and those who worship Him must worship in spirit and truth."

The human spirit is often referred to as the inner man or the real person within us and plays a vital role in our connection with God. Paul mentions this in the book of Romans, saying, "For I delight in the law of God in my inner being" (Romans 7:22). Here, he acknowledges that his true desire to follow God's law comes from his inner self, or spirit. He highlights that it is our inward man, or our spirit, that desires to do right and follow God's law.

The human spirit operates through three main functions: **Communion, Conscience, and Intuition.**

Communion

The primary function of the human spirit is communion with God. Many people struggle to hear from God because they attempt to do so without connecting spiritually, forgetting that God is a spirit. While the Bible confirms that people have heard God audibly, intimate communion takes place within our spirit. It is within this area of the human spirit that we worship God.

This sacred space of communion is free from external distractions. As stated in John 4:24," God is a spirit: and they that worship him must worship him in spirit and in truth." Since God is a spirit, the only way to truly worship Him is in your spirit. This place allows for complete honesty, vulnerability, and transparency, where worship is genuine and sincere.

The Conscience

Conscience can be defined as an inner sense of what is right and wrong in one's conduct or motives, impelling one toward right action. It acts as a moral compass, providing an internal guide to ethical behavior and helping individuals discern and feel conviction regarding their actions, thoughts, and decisions.

Our conscience is one of the functions of our human spirit. The conscience provides us with moral consciousness, the ability to discern between right and wrong. It functions as the place of conviction, even before we are born again. For instance, when we were younger and our parents told us not to do something, our conscience would bother us if we disobeyed, even if they did not yet know about it. This internal conviction occurs because the conscience acts as an internal detector of right and wrong, ensuring that we have no excuse for our actions.

God designed the conscience to work independently of our mind and reasoning. The conscience does not agree with sin and wrongdoing; however, it can be overruled by our will. When we choose to sin, it is because our will has dominated the conscience.

Additionally, the conscience can become seared or desensitized, The Holy Spirit, spoken through Timothy, warned that, in the last days, seducing spirits would cause people to give ear to doctrines of devils. "Speaking lies in hypocrisy, having their conscience seared with a hot iron" (1 Timothy 4:2), leading to a lack of sensitivity to right and wrong.

Intuition

The final function of the human spirit that we will discuss is intuition. One definition of intuition is the ability to understand something immediately, without the need for conscious reasoning. It is often described as a gut feeling or an instinctive response that guides decision-making and problem-solving without deliberate analytical thought.

In the complex interplay between soul and spirit, it can sometimes be challenging to determine which functions belong to each. The soul, spirit, and body of a person work so closely together that their functions may appear blurred. Intuition is one such function that can straddle the line between soul and spirit. It is essential to recognize that, while all parts of a person are interlinked and work together, they each have specific roles and positions within our three dimensional worlds.

11. THE NATURAL MINDSET

In the context of 1 Corinthians 2:14 ("The natural man receive not the things of the Spirit of God: for they are foolishness unto him: neither can he know them, because they are spiritually discerned"), it is clear that the natural mind is not equipped to grasp spiritual truths without divine illumination.

A natural-minded person is not necessarily a sinful-minded person. However, they can become sinful minded when natural thoughts dominate their thinking, leading to obsession or thoughts contrary to God's will. "Natural-minded" simply means that our focus and perspectives are more grounded in the tangible, physical world, often at the expense of our relationship with God.

The example of Martha and Mary from Luke 10:38-42 is a great one to illustrate this balance. In this story, while both women are doing good and necessary tasks, Jesus points out that Mary has chosen "what is better" because she prioritizes listening to His teachings. Martha's concern with serving and hospitality, though valuable, distracts her from the more crucial spiritual nourishment that Jesus offers.

In John 20:24-29, Thomas, one of Jesus 'twelve disciples, struggles to believe in Jesus 'resurrection. He famously states, "Unless I see the nail marks in His hands and put my finger where the nails were, and put my hand into His side, I will not believe" (John 20:25). Thomas's doubt can be understood as that of a naturally minded person; he witnessed Jesus's crucifixion, a deeply traumatic event, making it hard for him to naturally comprehend the miracle of the resurrection without physical proof.

From that moment, many changed his name to Doubting Thomas. However, Jesus, in His grace, appears to Thomas and invites him to touch His wounds, saying, "Stop doubting and believe" (John 20:27). Thomas responds with a profound declaration of faith, "My Lord and my God!" (John 20:28). In this moment, Thomas transitions from a natural-minded doubter to a spiritually-minded person full of faith.

The solution for the natural mind is not to be self-centered and to surrender to the will of God. Accept that you cannot understand spiritual things with logic. Understand that God's ways are not like your ways and His thoughts are not like your thoughts. God will not violate your right to think; however, he will not accept any thoughts that violate His way of thinking.

12. THE CARNAL MINDSET

The carnal mind is dominated by selfishness; it is self-centered, self-willed, self-serving, and self-focused. "The carnal mind is at enmity against God: for it is not subject to the law of God, nor indeed can be. So then: those who are in the flesh cannot please God" (Romans 8:7). To be at enmity against God means to be at war with God.

"Carnal" usually refers to being related to or governed by the physical or material appetites rather than spiritual or higher intellectual interests. It is often used to describe behavior or mindset that is worldly, sinful, or based on mere human desires, rather than on moral or spiritual values.

Paul writes to the Corinthians, "I, brethren, could not speak to you as unto spiritual, but as unto carnal, even as unto babes in Christ. I have fed you with milk, and not with meat: for hitherto ye were not able to bear it, neither yet now are ye able. For you are yet carnal for whereas there is among you envying and strife, and divisions; are ye not carnal and walk as men?" (1 Corinthians 3:1-3)

The following are areas of the carnal mind found in the scripture above:

The Solution for the carnal-minded person is listed below.

- Repent for being at war with God

- Surrender to God's way of thinking (God's word)

- Cultivate a prayer life

- Submit to the people in authority in your life

- Cast down every imagination that is contrary to the will of God

- Bring your thoughts into captivity to the word of God

- Let go of condemnation for being carnal-minded

13. THE WICKED MINDSET

The wicked mindset can be understood as a condition where an individual's thoughts and actions are heavily influenced by Satan's intents and behaviors, whose objective is to kill, steal, and destroy. This mindset represents a deeper level of moral corruption compared to the natural and carnal minds, but it is not beyond the reach of repentance and transformation through divine intervention. Listed below are scriptures to prove the wicked have an opportunity to repent.

- Let the wicked forsake his way, and the unrighteous man his thought; let him return to the Lord, that he may have compassion on him, and to our God, for he will abundantly pardon. (Isaiah 55:7).

- If my people who are called by my name humble themselves and seek my face and turn from their wicked ways, then will I hear from heaven and heal the land (2 Chronicles 7:14).

- Have I any pleasure in the death of the wicked, declares the Lord God, and not rather that he should turn from his way and live? (Ezekiel 18:23).

The solution for the wicked-minded person is to repent, turn from their wicked ways. This person may need to seek leadership to assist them, depended upon the areas of wickedness that they submitted themselves to.

14. THE REPROBATE MINDSET

People with a reprobate mindset choose to follow their own thoughts over the thoughts of God. Romans 1:28 says: "And even as they did not like to retain God in their knowledge, God gave them over to a reprobate mind, to do those things which are not convenient." This means that after people continuously reject God's truth, God allows them to follow their corrupted minds as a form of judgment.

Such people cannot repent; the Holy Spirit no longer gives them conviction. Satan has influence over the wicked-minded and the reprobate-minded person. The wicked-minded person can repent, but not the reprobate-minded person because such people are given over to the reprobate mind.

Consider that God gave them over to a reprobate mind. God, full of love and wanting the best for everyone, allows a person to be given over only after they have repeatedly rejected Him. This act is a form of divine judgment that we cannot change. A reprobate mind is no longer just dealing with temptation—it has been handed over to the individual's own evil thoughts and desires.

The Irreversibility of the Reprobate Mind:

Satan himself embodies both the wicked and the reprobate mindsets. His inability to repent stems not only from his wickedness but, more importantly, from his reprobate state. Similarly, those with a reprobate mind are described in the Bible as beyond the point of redemption, as they have been abandoned to their own evil devices.

Often, when the topic of a reprobate mind is discussed, people may feel anxious, fearing that they themselves might have such a mind. Sometimes it is even referred to as the unpardonable sin. However, it's important to understand that a reprobate mind is characterized by a conscious decision to reject God and a deliberate choice to pursue wickedness. This condition results from persistently turning away from righteousness and embracing evil, rather than committing a one-time mistake or suffering a moment of doubt.

Solution THERE IS NO SOLUTION FOR THE REPROBATE MIND!!!!

15. THE LOCKED MINDSET

A locked mindset refers to a way of thinking that is closed, fixed, and resistant to change. This type of mindset can develop for various reasons: either as a protective mechanism, through unconscious decisions, or simply out of stubbornness. However, understanding how a mindset becomes locked and how to unlock it is crucial for personal growth and development.

A Locked Mindset is primarily locked in four ways:

1. Rejection of Knowledge: A person who refuses to seek or accept knowledge risks stagnation. The Bible cautions against this in Hosea 4:6: "My people are destroyed for lack of knowledge: because thou hast rejected knowledge, I will also reject thee." When knowledge and truth are rejected, the growth that accompanies them is also rejected.

2. Stubborn Determination: Some individuals stubbornly cling to their ways of thinking, refusing to change. This stubbornness can trap their thinking process, making it resistant to development and new perspectives. Being locked in by stubbornness is akin to being self-willed.

3. Traumatic Experiences: Trauma can also lock a mindset, making it difficult for a person to change how they think. Unresolved traumatic experiences—such as death, sickness, and many other things in life that can traumatize a person—can create mental barriers that are hard to overcome without intentional effort and healing..

4. Satanic Influence:" The god of this world has blinded the minds of the them which believe not, lest the light of the glorious gospel of Christ, who is the image of God, should shine unto them" (2 Corinthians 4:4). This spiritual blindness can lock a mindset, preventing individuals from seeing truth and receiving deliverance.

A locked mindset has set rules that do not change. Unless intentional changes are made, the thoughts and mental pictures will stay the same, the end result is a repeat of old thoughts that bring hurt, disappointments, and unforgiveness that hinder freedom if our thinking is trapped in fear, doubt, unbelief, traumatic experiences, and negative thoughts.

If negative thoughts are not changed, they become voices that can only speak from its library of words, experiences, emotions, fears, beliefs, and any negative influences that we have accepted. If we want transformation, the locked mindset must be unlocked by the word of God: "Let this mind be in you, which was also in Christ Jesus" (Philippians 2:5).

Look at the following list to highlight areas you need change

1. Negative self-talk: Constantly repeating negative or limiting beliefs to oneself can reinforce a fixed mindset. For example, telling oneself "I can't do it" or "I'm not good enough."

2. Fear of failure: A fear of failure can prevent individuals from taking risks or stepping out of their comfort zones. This fear can lead to a reluctance to try new things or pursue challenging goals, ultimately keeping the mindset locked in place.

3. Comparison to others: Constantly comparing oneself to others can breed feelings of inadequacy and foster a fixed mindset. When individuals believe they can never measure up to others, they may resign themselves to staying stuck in their current situation.

4. Past experiences: Past experiences of failure, rejection, or criticism can shape a person's mindset and lead them to believe that they are incapable of growth or change. These experiences can create mental barriers that hold individuals back from reaching their full potential.

5. Limited beliefs: Holding onto limiting beliefs about oneself, such as "I'm not smart enough," "I'm not talented," or "I don't deserve success," can reinforce a fixed mindset and prevent personal growth.

6. External influences: Messages from family, friends, or society that reinforce a fixed mindset can further solidify locked patterns of thinking. When individuals are surrounded by negative influences or unsupportive environments, it can be challenging to break free from a fixed mindset.

16. THE TREE OF KNOWLEDGE

Unlocking mindset traps involves both receiving and refusing knowledge. Everything we have discussed, our thoughts and behaviors, is driven by words and images, all of which are products of some form of information. The mind is formed, woven by experiences and emotions, and fed by information.

We are in an information age, a time when information has become a commodity, spreading quickly and widely. Information is easily accessible; almost everyone has a phone or computer, tapping into worldwide information within seconds. As information has increased, it becomes crucial to understand the information we are receiving.

Information is important, but, remember, it's only data about someone or something obtained from various sources, such as a newspaper or the Internet, which stem from the voices of people, God, or the Devil; those are the only voices on Earth that speak in some form. Our mindset creates a mental voice shaped by what we allow to stay on our mind; this information then sets the course of our thinking process.

Information is different from knowledge. Information is data collected, while knowledge is the understanding and interpretation of information. If we operate only on information, then we have collected data about something but have not processed it in order to understand it and get a proper interpretation of the information we received.

An example of this is gossip. To someone who receives it, hearing negative information about another person can be thrilling. And such knowledge can puff up the ego, making that person feel superior to the person discussed. This gossip can be true or false; however, we need to process information to gain understanding and accurate knowledge to determine making decisions and what to do with information we receive.

Eve found this out when she was deceived by the serpent, saying, "God doth know that in the day ye eat thereof, then your eyes shall be opened, and ye shall be as gods, knowing good and evil" (Genesis 3:5).

Satan used misinformation to deceive Adam and Eve into disregarding the instructions given to them by God, which was not to eat from the tree of the knowledge of good and evil. Satan manipulated the instructions and convinced them not to retain the instructions God gave them. Every temptation we face will involve information to hinder our understanding and thinking, presenting misleading information to entice us to act against divine instruction. This example illustrates how misinformation can influence decisions and actions by distorting the perceived knowledge.

Information does not come from something; it comes from someone. If that someone is inaccurate or deceptive, and you accept their information, then you are inaccurate and have been deceived. I refuse to entertain some information; whether it's true or false, it's just a waste of time—what is my motive for being involved? My involvement should be to protect the vulnerable person and look for ways to reconcile and expose Satan's tactics.

True knowledge is formed from facts, gained through experience from reliable and trustworthy sources. To develop a sound mind, we must progress beyond simply acquiring information for its own sake. It is important to strive for an understanding grounded in truth, as highlighted in 2 Timothy 3:7: "Ever learning, and never able to come to the knowledge of the truth."

1. Stop and think about the way you think; where did it originate?

2. What portion of your thinking is not God's plan for you?

3. Do you really examine scripture to confirm what you believe?

Wisdom's Warnings: Areas of Misapplication of Knowledge

1. **The first area is we are destroyed for a lack of knowledge**. Not seeking knowledge

can destroy our purpose and every area of our lives. We cannot use the excuse "I did not know"; we are responsible to pursue knowledge. "My people are destroyed for **lack of knowledge**; Because you have **rejected knowledge**, I will reject you" (Hosea 4:6).

2. **<u>The second area is rejecting knowledge</u>**; The consequence is that, when you reject God's knowledge, you are rejecting God. How many people have been given knowledge of who God is, His love for them, and how He can change their lives— not only today but by giving them eternal life—and they reject it? If they continue to reject God's knowledge, which can give them eternal life, God will not violate the persons' will; he will reject them.

3. **<u>The third area:</u>** When you do not retain God in your knowledge, the consequence is a reprobate mind, as seen in the book of Romans: "And even as they did not like to retain God in their knowledge, God gave them over to a reprobate mind, to do those things which are not convenient" (Romans 1:28).

We cannot walk with God without agreeing with His standard of thinking: "Can two walk together, except they be agreed?" (Amos 3:3)

The ultimate goal of knowledge should be wisdom. Information is the accumulation of data, while knowledge is the understanding and interpretation of information. Wisdom is the application of knowledge; wisdom is the principal thing. Therefore, get WISDOM!

17. THE FIVE SOURCES OF INFORMATION AND KNOWLEDGE

The mindset we have today was formed by information or knowledge we have retained, whether consciously or unconsciously. Where did you obtain this information and knowledge; who is talking to you? We will explore five sources of information and knowledge that can become voices, guiding us in one of two directions, towards either deception or success in our lives.

Source 1.) Knowledge from God

The first and most important source of information and knowledge is God's word. God's word has been proven and trustworthy. However, some people don't trust God or his knowledge through His words because they cannot see Him, or they base their past relationships on how they perceive God will treat them. For example, if someone views God as a father but had a horrible experience with their own father or never knew their father, this could hinder how they receive knowledge from God. Let's dismantle these concerns:

The first concern. I cannot see God.

God is a spirit; our communication with God is on a spiritual level and with words. However, many can share stories on how GOD IS REAL. Nature itself is proof of someone who thought about your every need and desire. A sun to give us light, even a moon for light by night. (Remember, in the beginning, there was no electricity.) God made sure we would never experience complete darkness.

The next concern, God does not love me.

God is clear about his thoughts toward us, spoken by Jeremiah, "I know the thoughts I think toward you, saith the Lord; thoughts of good, not evil to give you an expected end" (Jeremiah 29:11). An expected end is to receive what you were already thinking and believing.

The final concern, How does God speak to me? I want to hear Him.

The first way God spoke to man was as an audible voice in the Garden of Eden when He spoke to Adam and Eve. Many have heard God in an audible voice—Moses, for example, spoke to God face-to-face on Mount Sinai; however, this is not the daily process God uses to speak to everyone today.

The second way God speaks is through the Bible, consisting of Sixty-six books that were written despite the transcribers being beaten, imprisoned, and even killed trying to preserve it. God's words are so necessary that nothing can stop its printing and distribution worldwide.

The third way God speaks is in Prayer; prayer is how we build a personal relationship by communicating with God. You may sense an inner witness and confidence. This confidence is confirmation by way of your human spirit, confirmed by the Holy Spirit of God that he is speaking to you.

Prayer requires humility and transparency, which help to build confidence. As it is written: "And this is the confidence that we have in him, if we ask anything according to his will, he hear us: and, if we know that he hear us, whatsoever we ask, we know that we have the petitions that we desired of him" (1 John 5:14-15).

The Fourth way God speaks is through men and women of God. Developing a personal relationship with God first through prayer is crucial before one can fully benefit from the teachings of those called to share His word with understanding and revelation. Just as you need a teacher to understand subjects like science or English, you need a preacher and spiritual teacher to help you understand God's word. "How can they hear without a preacher, and how can a preacher preach unless God has sent him?" Although there have been false teachers and preachers who have manipulated and hurt many people, remember that, for every fake, there is someone genuinely striving to obey God and help others. Don't give up on God because of the failures of mankind.

God communicates through both teaching and prophetic words, whether written or spoken. Both forms are inspired by God. As Peter confirmed, "For the prophecy came not in old time by the will of man: but holy men of God spoke as they were moved by the Holy Ghost" (2 Peter 1:21). The Word of God goes beyond mere information; it provides profound knowledge. Despite centuries of attempts to suppress it, through burning and bans, it has endured the test of time. These examples assure us that God truly desires to speak to us.

The Apostle John was exiled to the island of Patmos

The Apostle John was exiled to the island of Patmos as a consequence of preaching the Word of God. The purpose of the exile was to isolate him from those who could hear his message, thereby separating him from his community and family as a form of punishment.

While on the island, instead of yielding to loneliness, fear, and anger, John embraced his purpose and wrote the book of Revelation. What was meant for evil in John's exile to the Island of Patmos was turned for good because John loved God and John was called according to God's purpose to the island. (as stated in Romans 8:28: "And we know that all things work together for good to them that love God, to them who are called according to His purpose"). Therefore, John chose to obey God and write, thus fulfilling his divine mission. The book of revelation is a prophetic release of future events that gives us confidence that we win.

Whatever problem is in your life, God wants to work together on it with you for your own good. If all you see is the problem—look again.

There were many who released the word of God regardless of persecution. **The Apostle Paul** was put in jail for speaking God's words. Satan assumed this would stop him. I can imagine Paul sitting in a cell, looking out at a guard wearing physical armor, and saw spiritually that armor was also needed in **Physical, Spiritual** and **Mental battles.**

Paul writes, "Put on the whole armor of God that ye may be able to stand against the wiles of the devil" (Ephesians 6:11). Paul proceeds to write while watching the armor of the soldier. The Helmet of Salvation, the Breastplate of Righteousness. Paul illustrates spiritual weapons from the natural armor, as we discussed earlier. Paul was imprisoned to stop God's word, and the whole time God's word was being written to release men and women for thousands of years to come.

God's word will be released from every platform in these last days. I believe books will be released from the mouth of God through the hands of writers. The bible is already written, so these books will confirm and release revelation of the coming king. These books will give understanding, wisdom, and strategy from deliverance to finances, to preserve our families through every obstacle.

Life and changing times may make you think you're defeated, but do not be deceived: God has words that will give clarity and wisdom concerning your future.

Source 2.) Satan's Information

The second source of information is Satan's, which is full of deception. Satan is a thief; his thoughts and purpose are threefold. "The thief cometh not, but for to **steal**, and to **kill,** and to **destroy**" (John 10:10).

Satan's desire to exalt himself was so delusional that he thought he could steal God's position, kill Jesus, and destroy God's plan for man.

When Satan spoke to Eve, his purpose was to steal, kill, and destroy the relationship between her, Adam, and God. The relationship between God and a married couple is called a covenant. Satan understands the power of unity within a covenant and knows that God is a covenant keeper. By destroying the relationship between a person and God, and then between a husband and wife, Satan disrupts two levels of covenant. This allows him to plant generational curses that can affect families for centuries.

Let's first identify the deceptive information Satan gave Eve and, secondly, identify his purpose.

Deceptive Information: "God does know that in the day you eat"—this insinuates that God is hiding something from you, that God is afraid of you advancing.

Deceptive Information:" Your eyes shall be opened" insinuates that God is hiding something from Eve and has limited her knowledge.

Deceptive Information: "You will be as Gods, knowing good and evil" insinuates you will be equal to God; this appeals to pride.

Eve received deceptive information from the serpent, leading her to eat the forbidden fruit. She then gave the fruit to Adam, who, despite knowing God's command, chose to disobey. This highlights an important lesson: never compromise God's word for anyone. The god of this world seeks to blind the minds of people, preventing them from believing the glorious gospel.

"The God of this world, has blinded the minds of the people lest they would believe the glorious gospel" (2 Corinthians 4:4).

Source 3.) We Are the Source of the Information

The third source of information is our own thoughts, will, desires and our five senses. I want to repeat that we are tripart beings, spirit, soul, and body, to give more clarity. The way mankind is compartmentalized, you are a spirit, you have a soul, and you live in a body. The information we receive does not have to come from God or Satan; it can simply be the way we choose to think.

The three parts of man receive information from three different realms. The Spirit Realm, The Soulish Realm and the Physical Realm. I know we are discussing mindset traps, however information from the three parts of man does influence every part of mankind.

The spirit of man can desire time with God.

The soul of man (will, mind, emotions) can desire to be stubborn or logical (I am tired).

The physical can submit to the five senses like Thomas doubting unless I see, touch I will not believe.

Source 4.) Adopted Information

The fourth source of information is to adopt the way someone else thinks. One definition of word *adopt* is to legally take on parenthood of a child you did not birth. Another definition of adoption is to follow an idea, method, or course of action, to take on or assume an attitude or position that's not your own but belongs to someone else.

When you adopt someone's ideas, thoughts, and way of doing things, you are aware of your choice. You take on this behavior not by association but by choice. For example, "Let this mind be in you which was also in Christ Jesus" (Philippians 2:5); you can adopt this mindset. We purposely take on how Jesus thinks and behaves; we adopted it by choice.

We can also adopt (choose) corrupt behavior, "Be not deceived: evil communications corrupt good manners" (1 Corinthian 15:33). How we think and we behave is evidence of the source we are getting information from and whose lifestyle we have adopted.

Source 5.) Adapted Information

The fifth source you receive information from is **adapting** to another person's thoughts. To adapt is for a person to adjust him or herself to changing or getting used to a new situation or circumstance. **Adapting can be by choice but normally come from a requirement or a compromise to continue in an environment.**

When adapting is a requirement, it's to incorporate us into a better position for living, a job, or relationships. If you move from California to New York, you will have to adapt to this change of environment, culture, and mindset; this is a required adaptation to develop.

Adapting as a compromise is lowering your standards in a certain environment. An example of this compromise is seen in Galatians 2:11-12, when Paul confronts Peter to his face for hypocrisy, secretly eating with the Gentiles behind the back of the Jews because they were not circumcised, creating a division when Paul was teaching to bring unity with the Gentiles and the Jews.

We can see from these two examples, of the Apostle John and Apostle Paul that God used these men to write and speak the sure words of prophecy, releasing God's word through the spoken word and the written word. It is important to know our source of information, knowledge, understanding to receive wisdom.

Authority figures can try to force you to adapt and adopt to a false doctrine, we do not have to submit. God definitely told us to, "Obey them that have the rule over us, and submit ourselves: for they watch for our souls" (Hebrews 13:17). This is not a license to lead you into false doctrine, or to violate you sexually, financially, or through any type of violation. The right people (such as authority figures, parents, spouses, counselors, pastors, teachers, and even a good friend) can be beneficial in giving good advice. "In the multitude of counselors there is safety" (Proverbs 11:14); just keep in mind we follow men as they follow Christ.

TEACHINGS OF DR. LAURETTA PICKETT

The Image Is in the Seed

This Trial Is Going to Bless Me

Being Caught Up

No More Excuses

Exposing the Spirit of Death

Anointed Healing Prayer

Single & Satisfied

Exposing Lust & Seducing Spirits

Deliverance For God's Woman

The Spirit of the Finisher

Season for a Breakthrough

Transforming the Mind

Called Without an Excuse

Understanding Dreams & Visions

Prophetic Clarity

Understanding The Spirit, Soul and Body